Preface

In **In life sometimes we find ourselves in a situation where we desperately need help,but no door seems open & no source of blessings seems working for us, & this is not the case a individual go through, but all of us might have experienced or would be experiencing this in our life, as no body knows what is in the box of present & future nothing is certain,what is certain are blessings ,support ,care ,love & guidance we can have ,which can further enable & strengthen us to face all these odds,Reiki is on of the purest & surest blessings we can have,if you are reading this book certainly you are on the path of Reiki & its blessings.**

Be healed & help others heal.

Table of Contents

The secret art of inviting happiness The miraculous medicine of all diseases Just for today, do not anger Do not worry and be filled with gratitude Devote yourself to your work. Be kind to people. Every morning and evening, join your hands in prayer. Pray these words to your heart and chant these words with your mouth Usui Reiki Treatment for the improvement of body and mind.

Dr .MIKAO USUI.

WHAT IS REIKI?

Reiki is a spiritual and divine healing technique, which heals at various levels like mental, physical, emotional and spiritual. It is based on the idea that an unseen "life force energy" flows through us and is what causes us to be alive. If one's "life force energy" is not balanced, then they are more likely to get sick or feel stress, and if it is balanced, then we are more capable of being happy and healthy.

The word Reiki is made of two Japanese words - **Rei** which means "God's Wisdom or the Higher Power" and **Ki** which is "life force energy "which has been effective in helping virtually every known illness.

An amazingly simple technique to learn, the ability to use Reiki is neither comes from just teaching nor comes from reading about it various levels, but it is transferred to the student during a Reiki class. This ability is passed on during an "attunement" given by a Reiki master and allows the student to tap into an unlimited supply of "life force energy" which never runs out and helps to improve one's health and enhance the quality of life.

REI = Spirit or Spiritual

KI = Universal Life Force Energy

Who can do Reiki

- Anybody can do Reiki who believes that there is a life force energy as it is very simple, effective, natural and safe method of spiritual healing.
- Not only health but also for self-improvement everyone can use Reiki
- Its use is not dependent on one's intellectual capacity or spiritual development and therefore is available to everyone.
- While Reiki is spiritual in nature, it is not a religion.

HOW REIKI WORKS

- Reiki re-establishes a normal flow of energy (Ki) within the body to heal all levels – physical, emotional, mental and spiritual (Note: life-force energy is also known as Chi/Qi [China], Prana [India] or Huna [Hawaii]

- Our physical body is sensitive to the energy of thoughts and emotions. When we experience negative feelings or thoughts about ourselves, develop negative thought patterns and beliefs, or experience a physical or emotional shock, this affects our energy field, creating emotional and physiological blockages that eventually disrupt our health

- Reiki frees and aligns the body's energy system, which in turn releases pain on all levels – physical, emotional, mental and spiritual.

- Reiki aids the body in releasing *stress* and tension by creating deep relaxation and it restores energy balance and vitality by relieving the physical and emotional effects of unreleased stress.

- It gently and effectively opens blocked meridians (energy pathways) and chakras (energy centers) and clears the energy bodies, leaving you feeling relaxed and at peace

- For Reiki is more effective, the client should be open minded and willing to take responsibility to alter negative life patterns or issues to create their own healing

- Reiki is simple and provides measurable results - in essence, it is power, light and love

HISTORY OF REIKI-

Healing at the level of life force energy was discovered by Gautama Buddha 2500 years ago, "Jesus Christ" and "Sai Baba" were capable of healing people with their touch and intention.

The devotees of Gautama Buddha were also capable of healing people with touch called "BaudhaAussadhi"
Reiki was rediscovered in the mid 1800's by a Japanese born Buddhist monk, Dr. MikaoUsui. While teaching in a college, Dr. Usui was asked by a student how Jesus facilitated the healing miracles that he performed. The question had planted a seed and set Dr. Usui out on the path to answer 'that question'. Dr. Usui was determined to learn the secret healing so that he may help others and his journey took him to many countries.

He studied book "Kamal sutra" and "Buddhadarshan Shastra" in a math in Tibet and was highly inspired by the healing technique of Gautama Buddha.

1. Dr MIKAO USUI (PRONOUNCED MICK-COW EW-SUEY)

- MikaoUsui was born August 15, 1865 in Taniai village (now Miyama district), Japan

- The title of "doctor" as you may find written in many modern Reiki books, was an entitlement adopted by the Western interpretation of his humble beginnings; he was not a medical physician.

- It is believed that Mikao Usui practiced as a Tendai Buddhist priest, as well as a Shugenja (pronounced Shoe-Gen-ja; translated from Japanese means one with magical powers such as a medium, fortune-teller, psychic or spiritual healer)

- Usui studied and practiced TendaiMikkyo Buddhism (pronounced Ten-die Meek-key-o), Shintoism (pronounced Shin-toe-is-im; a Japanese faith worshipping objects of worship called kami), martial arts and Shugendo. It is believed that his vast knowledge learned from these practices influenced and formalized his spiritual-based teaching method

- He was a member of an association called Rei Jutsu Kai (pronounced Ray-jut-sue Kye), which was known for its spiritual teachers who used a Japanese form of palm-healing, called tenohira (pronounced ten-oh-here-a) to heal others and it is thought that this form of palm-healing is the precursor of what is known as Reiki today. Usui healed in an intuitive manner, allowing himself to be guided through his inner senses.

- In 1922, he went to the sacred mountain of Mt. Kurama (pronounced Cure-am-a), where as part of his spiritual practice, he fasted and meditated for 21 days before receiving divine inspiration for the Reiki symbols and how they worked.

- In April 1922, he opened a clinic/school in Harajuku, Aoyama, Tokyo offers his spiritual system of healing techniques called Usui Reiki Ryoho, or also Usui Shiki Ryoho

- In 1925, he opened a larger clinic/school in Nakano, outside of Tokyo.

- On March 9th, 1926, Mikao Usui passed from a stroke. He is buried in the Saihoji Temple in Suginami-Ku, Tokyo, where a memorial is erected honoring his life's work and contribution.

- Before his death, He initiated 16 Usui Shiki Ryoho Masters, (Usui Shiki Ryoho translated means Usui Style Healing), one of whom was a retired naval officer DrChujiro Hayashi who continued it thereafter.

"All healing is first a healing of the heart." - Carl Townsend

DR. CHUJIRO HAYASHI (PRONOUNCED CHEW-JEER-OH HI-ASH-EE)

- Chujiro Hayashi was born in September 15, 1878 in Tokyo, Japan

- He was formally trained as a naval officer, plus also a naval surgeon in 1902

- In 1925, at age 47, he received Shinpiden from MikaoUsui. (Shinpiden translated means the mystery/secret teachings, equivalent to Reiki Master Teacher Level)

- He was instrumental in organizing the first Reiki manual showing hand positions, symbols, body diagrams and illnesses

- Hayashi broke away to develop his own modified system of Reiki after Usui's death and opened his own commercial clinic for paying clients at a small clinic in Tokyo named Hayashi Reiki Kenkyu-kai

- On May 10th, 1941, because Hayashi was a man of peace, he felt that he could not participate in WWII, so he committed suicide (Seppuku) in the presence of his wife and students

- Before his death, Hayashi initiated 17 Shinpiden Masters, (Shinpiden translated means the mystery/secret teachings, equivalent to Reiki

Master Teacher Level), including his wife Chie Hayashi and Hawaii Takata

HAWAYO TAKATA (PRONOUNCED HAH-WHY-OH TAA-KAA-TA)

- HawayoTakata was born HawayoKawamuru, December 24, 1900 in Hanamaulu, Kauai, Hawaii (pronounced Hana-maul-la, Kah-why-ee)

- She married SaichiTakata March 10, 1917, but was widowed October, 1930.

- Mrs. Takata apparently suffered from severe abdominal pain and while visiting Japan, she met Churjiro Hayashi (pronounced Chew-jeer-oh Hi-ash-ee) at his Reiki clinic in Shina-No-Machi, Tokyo, where after 4 months, her health was restored and thus prompted her keen interest to learn Reiki.

- In the spring of 1936 Takata received Shoden from Chujiro Hayashi. (Pronounced Show-den; translated means the entrance, equivalent to Reiki Level 1).

- In 1937 Takata received Okuden from Chujiro Hayashi and then returned to Hawaii to open the first foreign Reiki healing clinic in Kapaa, Hawaii. (Pronounced Oh-koo-den; translated means the deep inside, it's equivalent to Reiki Level 2).

- February 21, 1938, Takata received Shinpiden from Hayashi in Hawaii, where he announced HawayoTakata as a Reiki Master, plus his successor. (Pronounced Ship–i–den; translated means the mystery/secret teachings, equivalent to Reiki Master Teacher Level).

- It is thought that Takata Sensei introduced a Western version of how MikaoUsui discovered Reiki, plus she set up her own price structure and teaching system.

- Takata Sensei brought Reiki to mainland North America where she taught Levels 1 and 2 in the United States and Canada, but did not teach Master Level until the 1970's.

- Students paid Takata $10,000 USD for Reiki Master Teacher level, plus they apprenticed for 1-year. Takata's exorbitant fee created much controversy, for to put this into proper perspective, in the 1970's, $10,000 USD would buy a house in the US.

- From 1970-1980, Takata initiated 22 Usui Shiki Ryoho Reiki Masters. (Usui Shiki Ryoho; translated means Usui Style Healing).

- On December 11, 1980, HawayoTakata passed away from a heart attack.
- . It is from these original masters that Reiki had spread in the world outside of Japan.

"Healing takes courage, and we all have courage, even if we have to dig a little to find it." - Tori Amos

Usui Reiki Ryoho is also known by other names:

Usui Shiki Ryoho (translated from Japanese means Usui style healing)

UsuiReiho (translated from Japanese means Usui Spiritual Method

Usui Do (translated from Japanese means Usui Spiritual Path)

UsuiTeate (translated from Japanese means Usui Treatment.

Today, Reiki has been expanded and diversified under various names, but One Source continues to teach the original three level format known today as Usui Shiki Ryoho.

- As Reiki continues to evolve, in all its variations, it is becoming more widely known and been accepted as a valuable healing method that supports, compliments and benefits the alternative healing arts, as well as conventional Western medicine by promoting gentle, non-evasive, rapid healing at all levels – mental, emotional, physical and spiritual.

I'm touched by the idea that when we do things that are useful and helpful - collecting these shards of spirituality - that we may be helping to bring about a healing." - Leonard Nimoy

REIKI PRINCIPLES

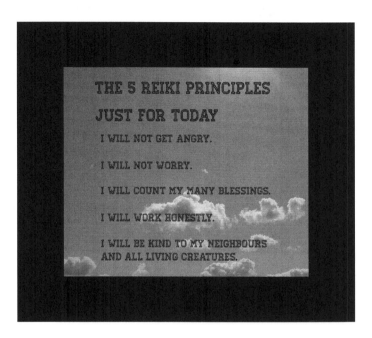

I - Just for today, I will not be angry.

- Anger at others or at self or at the entire world, creates serious blockages in one's energy. It is the most complex inner enemy.
- Reiki is an excellent tool to remove anger blockages which have accumulated in the body over years, but it cannot remove the residue of current anger which occurs daily.
- Letting go of anger brings Piece into the Mind.

II - Just for today, I will not worry.

- While anger deals with past and present events, worry deals with future ones. Although worry is not always a negative phenomenon, endless worries may fill one's head, and each one bores a small hole in one's body and soul.
- While anger requires a focused Reiki treatment to remove obstacles, worry requires the energy to be spread throughout the entire body.
- Letting go of worry, brings healing in the Body.

III - Just for today, I will be grateful.

- Be grateful from your hart inward. Inner intention is the important element in this principle. Simple things as thanks, forgiveness, smile, good words, gratitude can improve others life and make them happy.
- Being thankful brings Joy into the Spirit.

IV - Just for today, I will do my work honestly.

- Support yourself and your family respectably, without harming others. Earn a respectable living, live a life of honor.

- Working honestly brings Abundance into the Soul.

V- Just for today, I will be kind to every living thing.

- Honor your parents, honor your teachers, and honor your elders.
- Being Kind brings Love into the Will.

REIKI BELIEFS

DrMikao Usui offered Reiki to everyone, but he soon realized that unless people were willing to take responsibility for their own well-being, they soon reverted to their former living environment or daily living habits and their previous health conditions would re-occur.

For people to participate and to appreciate their own healing, there must be an exchange of energy, so he implemented the following two beliefs. It is believed that these originate from his spiritual, as well as his martial arts training background.

- There must be a change in consciousness for healing to occur
- There must be an appropriate exchange of energy; one that honors' each

Today, if a person wishes to have a Reiki treatment, there must be an exchange between the practitioner and the client. This can be an exchange of services, goods or money, but it must be agreeable, plus be for the mutual benefit of both parties.

BENEFITS OF REIKI

Each person experiences Reiki in their own individual way, so it is important to be open to more than what is listed here.

- Balances the body's energy flow
- Beneficial for plants and animals
- Energizes and balances glands, bodily functions and strengthens the immune system
- Energizes body, mind and spirit
- Frees blocked emotions
- Frees blocked energy
- Increases creativity and awareness

- Increases serotonin and endorphins released by the brain to relieve pain
- Relaxes by working on the physical, emotional, mental and spiritual levels
- Releases toxins and impurities from the body
- Relieves stress
- Supports and activates the body's natural ability to heal itself
- Used for distant/absentee healing and healing the planet
- Used to heal past, present and future experiences
- Used to charge gemstone elixirs, medicines, herb tinctures, or homeopathic remedies
- Used to clear and charge crystals and gemstones
- Used to clear food and beverages of impurities

The Reiki curriculum offered, teaches three degrees or levels of traditional Reiki called Usui Shiki Ryoho (pronounced Ew-suey She-key Rye-oh-ho), a spiritual energy based healing method that uses unique symbols, which give each degree its own specific purpose. The Japanese translation of Usui Shiki Ryoho means Usui style healing.

First Degree (You Sense the Energy)

REIKI LEVEL 1 (also called the 1st degree), is the foundation of all levels

- This degree is permanent and remains with you during your entire life (even if you stop practicing Reiki) it cannot be reversed. Therefore, it is important that it is your decision to take the first degree and not allow someone else to decide on your behalf

- The main purpose of Reiki Level 1 is to learn about self-healing, which involves taking responsibility for your own health and well-being, After completing Reiki Level 1, you may also heal others, as well as animals freely or by donation for non-professional purposes, Through an attunement ceremony called Reiju (pronounced ray-joo), you are initiated by a Reiki Master Teacher to three Reiki symbols:

- This is done through four initiations that help you to facilitate and strengthen your connection to universal life force energy, allowing it to flow through you to raise your personal energy level. The Reiki symbols permanently remain within your aura and their energy emerges unconsciously through your hands.

WHAT IS INITIATION

In Japanese, this ceremony is called Reiju (pronounced Ray-joo) and translated, it means spiritual energy blessing. In a modern-day ceremony, your body moves into a spiritual state (or universal state) using ancient sounds or symbols, which harmonize your mental and emotional bodies, plus also aligns your spiritual essence within to re-connect you to your true "self" (or your soul). The attunement also clears your meridians (energy pathways) throughout your body to allow Ki (universal life force energy) to flow freely.

The Reiki Master Teacher does not have any special powers to pass along, but merely acts as a channel to provide or create a safe place for you to draw in Ki, thus allowing you to connect universal life force energy (Source, Divine) to your inner self or soul. You will draw Ki to the level where you specifically need it – mental, emotional, physical or spiritual levels.

By receiving attunement or Reiju at each Reiki level, you accept universal blessings to support your journey of self-responsibility for your own spiritual progress. Your success in your personal journey depends entirely on how much time and effort you are willing to apply; the more effort you make, the more blessings you receive.

The Purpose of Attunement The main purpose of an attunement is to raise your energy level to re-connect you to your inner true self (soul), plus strengthen your connection to universal spiritual energy. In Reiki Level 1 (also called 1st Degree); you are attuned through four initiations or Reiju, to 3 symbols – the power symbol, mental/emotional symbol and the distant/absentee symbol.

First Initiation (Head) - Energy is utilized through your physical body to raise your energy vibration level and to increase your healing capacity. It opens your crown to allow more universal light, wisdom and purpose.

Second Initiation (Shoulder) - Energy is utilized through your etheric body (your spiritual double located slightly above your physical body). It opens your cervical and spinal column to improve the functioning of your entire nervous system, plus opens your throat chakra to enhance better communication.

Third Initiation (Occipital) - Balances your right and left brain to induce clearer thinking and action.

Fourth Initiation (Forehead) - Influences your pineal and pituitary glands, which increases higher consciousness and intuition. This initiation completes the process, allowing the energy channels to remain open and seals the symbols into your aura.

"Healing may not be so much about getting better, as about letting go of everything that isn't you - all of the expectations, all of the beliefs - and becoming who you are." - Rachel Naomi Remen

Aura before/After attunement

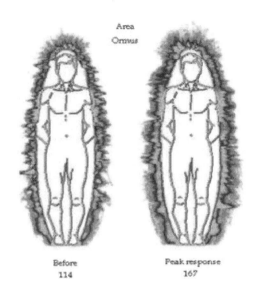

Area
Ormus

Before
114

Peak response
167

CLEANSING METHOD

Cleansing/Releasing - Method A

Starting from your Crown use both hands to dry brush your body with a downward sweeping motion until you brush your whole body (as if you are brushing dust off yourself)
With intention, visualize all impurities, negative energy and toxins leave your body through your foot chakras (soles of your feet) into the center core of

Mother Earth to be recycled or transformed into positive energy that will be used by the universe at the appropriate time

Cleansing/Releasing - Method B

- With intention, visualize yourself under a shower or a waterfall
- Visualize and feel the water washing and cleansing away all impurities, toxins and negative vibrations into the center core of Mother Earth to be recycled or transformed into positive energy that will be used by the Universe at the appropriate time.

Cleansing/Releasing - Method C

- Clear your mind of all thoughts
- Think of something calming and pleasant
- Shake your hands, then place them on an inanimate object
- With intention, visualize and allow all impurities, toxins and negative energy to drain out of your body through your hands and feet into the center core of Mother Earth

to be recycled or transformed into positive energy that will be used by the universe at the appropriate time

PROTECTION METHOD

Protection - Method A

- Close your eyes
- Take three deep breaths to relax your body
- With a prayer of intent, silently ask the universal source, "Please surround me in a dome (or column) of white (or golden) light to protect and ground me to the center core of Mother Earth"
- Then say, "I know that I am safe and secure at all times"
- Acknowledge your gratitude by saying, "Thank-you, thank-you, thank-you" (1st thank-you is to Source, 2nd thank-you is to your Spirit Healing Team, 3rd thank-you is to your soul or higher self)

Protection - Method B

- Close your eyes
- Take three deep breaths to relax your body
- With a prayer of intent, silently ask the universal source, "Please surround me in a bubble of rainbow colors that is also surrounded by a shield of reflecting mirrors that will deflect all negative energies, plus protect me at all times"
- Visualize this happening and feel and know that you are safe and secure always
- Acknowledge your gratitude by saying, "Thank-you, thank-you, thank-you" (1st thank-you is to Source, 2nd thank-you is to your Spirit Healing Team, 3rd thank-you is to your soul or higher self.

Protection - Method C

- Close your eyes
- Take three deep breaths to relax your body
- With a prayer of intent, ask your Spirit Healing Team, (which may include your guides, angels, DrMiakoUsui, etc.) to provide you with protection
- Feel and know that you are safe and secure at all times

- Acknowledge your gratitude by saying, "Thank-you, thank-you, thank-you" (1st thank-you is to Source, 2nd thank-you is to your Spirit Healing Team, 3rd thank-you is to your soul or higher self)

"The wish for healing has always been half of health." - Lucius Annaeus Seneca

GROUNDING METHOD

Grounding - Method A

- Close your eyes
- Take three deep breaths to relax your body
- With intent, visualize roots (like a tree) spreading from the base of your spine and foot to the center core of the earth
- Feel and know that you are fully grounded.

Grounding - Method B

- Close your eyes
- Take three deep breaths to relax your body
- With intent, visualize that you are inside a vacuum
- As your breath in feel the universal life force energy flow into you and fill you up like a balloon
- Feel yourself expand outward and upward
- Feel and know that you are fully grounded from the center core of the earth up into the universe.

I've experienced several different healing methodologies over the years - counseling, self-help seminars, and I've read a lot - but none of them will work unless you really want to heal." - Lindsay Wagner

WHAT IS AURA

- The aura is your energy identity. A swirling mass of colors it represents you on the mental, physical and emotional level. Your thoughts and feelings give color to your aura, making it possible for a psychic to know what you are experiencing. Although it is widely accepted that there are 7 levels of the aura, some psychics can perceive subtler levels. Healthy auras are markedly brighter and bigger, radiating a positivity and warmth that is tangible to everyone.

- Everything in the Universe seems to be just a vibration. Every atom, every part of an atom, every electron, every elementary "particle", even our thoughts and consciousness are just vibrations. Hence, we may define the Aura as a electro-photonic vibration response of an object to some external excitation

- Advanced spiritual people such as Buddha, Christ etc had Strong Auras.

- Aura around living (conscious) objects (people, plants ...) changes with time, sometimes very quickly. Aura around non-living object (stones, crystals, water...) is essentially fixed, but can be changed by our conscious intent. Above facts have been observed by scientists in Russia, who have been using Kirlian effect to study Auras for the last 50 years.

- Colors and intensity of the aura, especially around and above the head have VERY special meanings. Watching someone's aura you can see.

- Also, aura is our spiritual signature. When you see a person with a bright, clean aura, you can be SURE that such person is good and spiritually advanced, even if he/she is modest and not aware of it. When you see a person with a gray or dark aura, you may be almost SURE, that such person has unclear intentions, regardless how impressive, eloquent, educated, "good looking" or "well dressed" he/she seems to appear.

- By reading Aura it seems possible to diagnose malfunctions in the body (diseases) long before physical symptoms become evident. By consciously controlling your Aura you can heal yourself.

- However, healing of the physical body is nothing in comparison to what seeing and reading auras can do for our consciousness, spiritual development and our awareness of Nature.

- Everyone has an Aura. But most people on Earth have VERY WEAK and dull Auras. This seems to be a direct consequence of their lifelong materialistic attitude negating and suppressing the development of consciousness, cultivating fear, envy, jealousy and other similar emotions. Such attitude suppresses their True Nature, and their Auras seem to become suppressed too.

- Children have much cleaner and stronger auras than most of adults, who are usually completely enslaved by the materialistic world and suppress their Nature by following superficial examples. When I taught my 12-year-old son to see his own Aura, he told me that when he was little he was able to see Auras most of the time. But no one paid any attention, so he thought that it was not important and maybe there was something wrong with his eyesight. This is a typical scenario. In my opinion children should learn to see and read Auras in a primary school, so they never lose this natural ability.

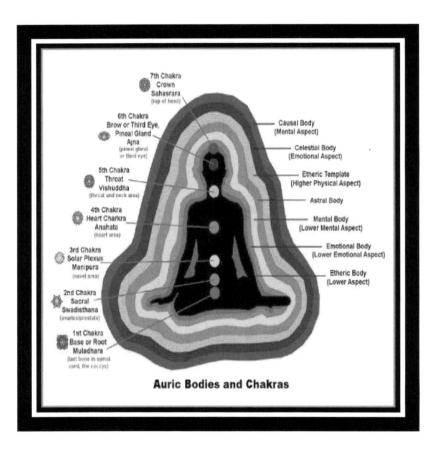

Auric Bodies and Chakras

KIRLIAN PHOTOGRAPHY OF AN AURA OF FINGERS

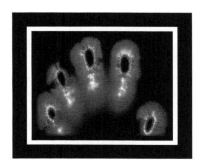

SELF AURA SCANNING

- To scan your own energy, simply follow the Self Treatment positions:
- Hold your non-dominant hand about 2 to 10 inches away from your body.
- Do one quick pass, trying to pay attention to the overall feel of your energy.
- Then do a second pass, this time noticing the subtle differences from place to place.
- An area may feel hotter (drawing energy in) or cooler (energy flowing out).
- Or perhaps it feels thicker or thinner, with your hand moving more slowly or faster through this space.

- There may be subtle vibrations that change from place to place. Again, this is all about 2 to 10 inches away from you (in the mental and emotional space).

These sensations usually indicate that the energy is either in a state of change, or needs some assistance. Next, apply Reiki in your aura with both hands wherever you felt something unusual or different. Just give Reiki for a minute or two in each place. When you are finished, begin a normal Reiki treatment on yourself. Notice if the Scanning and Reiki in the higher levels of the aura have made a difference in how you feel (mentally, emotionally, and physically). Over time you will become familiar with the energy feel of your aura and body.

HAND SCANNING THE AURA OF OTHERS

Step 1 - Before scanning

- Ground and protect yourself
- Attune yourself to your spiritual healing team (E.g. guides, angels, Dr. Mikao Usui, Reiki

Masters, Ascended Masters or universal source) asking for guidance and assistance

- Sensitize your hands by rubbing them together for 30 seconds and press the thumb of your opposite hand into the center chakra of each hand (this activates your hand chakras)
- With your client in a standing position, stand 4 meters (or 4 yards) away with your arms comfortably outstretched and your palms facing the client
- Slowly walk toward your client; concentrate on the center of your palms (without this concentration you will have difficulty scanning), while you simultaneously feel or scan your client's outer aura (energy field)
- Stop when you feel heat, tingling or pressure; you are now feeling the outer aura.

- Try feeling the following:
  1. Size and shape
  2. Width from head to waist
  3. Width from waist to feet
  4. Width from front to back

It may feel like an inverted egg with the top feeling wider than the bottom

To be more accurate, try to feel the pressure when determining the width or the outer, health and inner auras

Note: Aura Scanning can be done by L-ROD and Aura Scanner.

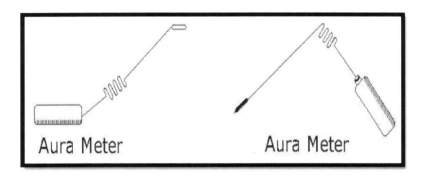

Aura Meter   Aura Meter

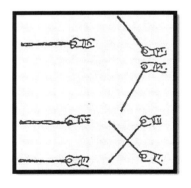
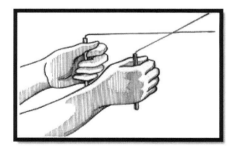

SCAN RESULTS

Hollows – this is caused from energy (Ki) depletion, which may be because of partial or severely blocked meridians (energy channels). The affected chakra is depleted and filled with dirty, diseased energy, resulting in the chakra becoming partially under-activated.

Congestion – this occurs when there is energy congestion (excess energy in a localized area) that partially or severely blocks the surrounding meridians (energy channels). Over time, since fresh energy cannot flow freely, the congested energy becomes devitalized and diseased. The affected chakra becomes congested and filled with diseased energy and then becomes partially over-activated.

Note: Disease first manifests within the energy body before manifesting on the physical body. If energy is applied before the disease manifests physically, this will usually result in a more positive and favorable recovery.

REASONS OF WEAK AURA

- Weakness, fatigue, exertion.
- Deficiency of fresh air.
- Addiction of any kind alcohol, drug, etc.
- Stress and anxiety.
- Nasty or psychic activity.
- Improper or poor diet.

Clean and healed aura can make you feel fresh, happy and lively. With a cleansed aura, you become sensitively stable and full of positive thoughts. It gives you positive energy to face the ups and downs of life

HOW TO MAKE YOUR AURA STRONG

- Drink more water, at least 9 to 12 glasses a day.
- Take warm water bath with rock salt, or one can even use normal salt if rock salt is not available.
- Wear clothes that make you feel happy like your favorite color.

- Sunbathe walking or standing in sunlight for a few minutes can also purify your aura.
- Blow of wind can also cleanse the aura. Walking or standing in the way of the wind is the best way to purify your aura. You just need to find a place where you can access fresh air with sunlight.
- Healing crystals and gemstones are also good cleansers; one can use the crystal that resonates with their energy.
- Conscious breathing exercise for five to 15 minutes is also helpful.
- Meditation and even reading spiritual books can make your Aura strong.

PREPARATION OF SELF FOR REIKI SELF-TREATMENT

- Wash your hands (for sanitary purposes)
- Relax in a comfortable position (sitting or lying down)
- Play soft, relaxing music if you wish
- You can make place sacred, by lightening incense stick or camphor lamp.
- Wear loose, comfortable clothing

- Remove watches and jewelry or metal objects (okay to leave wedding rings on if you wish)
- Ground and protect yourself
- Set your intent – remember, it is your focus and intention that starts the Reiki energy flowing

Examples:

1. To heal your illness or disease
2. To release pain, stiffness or discomfort
3. To remove energy blockages from past or present issues
4. To release toxins and impurities from your body
5. To cleanse and balance your body
6. To energize your body.

   Silently state a simple invocation – remember, thoughts are energy and action always follows a thought

"Healing yourself is connected with healing others." - Yoko Ono

Examples:

1. Let Reiki flow for the highest and greatest good
2. To be a clear channel for Reiki universal life force energy
3. Ask for assistance from your Spirit Healing Team (which may include your guides, angels, Ascended Masters/teachers, Dr. Mikao Usui, other Reiki Masters or universal source)

- Begin your self-treatment hand positions holding for 3-5 minutes at each position or follow your intuition and do what you are guided to do
- When finished, cleanse yourself using the dry brush method or shower method, etc. (to disconnect your energy from your Spirit Healing Team)
- Say a silent prayer of gratitude
- Wash your hands (for sanitary purposes and to remove excess contaminated energy lingering in your system)

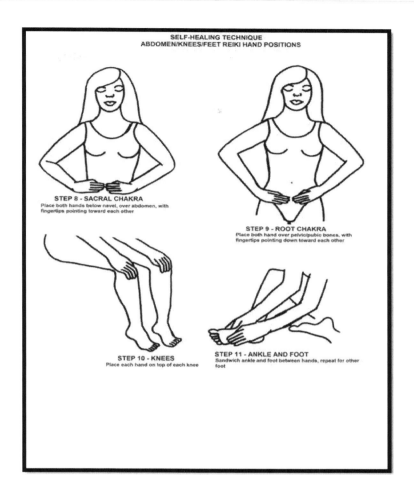

SELF-HEALING TECHNIQUE
ABDOMEN/KNEES/FEET REIKI HAND POSITIONS

STEP 8 - SACRAL CHAKRA
Place both hands below navel, over abdomen, with fingertips pointing toward each other

STEP 9 - ROOT CHAKRA
Place both hand over pelvic/pubic bones, with fingertips pointing down toward each other

STEP 10 - KNEES
Place each hand on top of each knee

STEP 11 - ANKLE AND FOOT
Sandwich ankle and foot between hands, repeat for other foot

SELF-HEALING TECHNIQUE
BACK OF HEAD/SHOULDERS
REIKI HAND POSITIONS

STEP 12 - CROWN
Cup hands over top of head with fingertips pointing toward each other, leaving a space for energy flow

STEP 13 - BACK OF HEAD
Place hands at back of head, with fingertips pointing toward each other or with one hand placed above the other hand

STEP 14 - BACK OF NECK
Reach over top of shoulders to place hands at top of shoulder blades, with fingertips pointing downward. If you have difficulty reaching, then place hands however far they can reach

STEP 15 - MIDDLE OF BACK
Reach behind to place hands over middle back ribs, below shoulder blades/back of the heart area, with fingertips pointing toward each other. If you have difficulty reaching, then place hands however far they reach

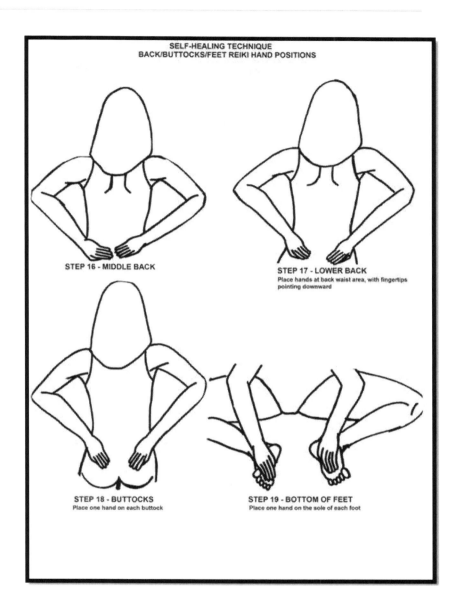

SELF-HEALING TECHNIQUE
BACK/BUTTOCKS/FEET REIKI HAND POSITIONS

STEP 16 - MIDDLE BACK

STEP 17 - LOWER BACK
Place hands at back waist area, with fingertips pointing downward

STEP 18 - BUTTOCKS
Place one hand on each buttock

STEP 19 - BOTTOM OF FEET
Place one hand on the sole of each foot

Week 1 - Hand Positions for the 21-day Cleansing Process

Week 1 Daily Exercise			
Day	Hands	Chakra	Minutes
1	Both hands on	Root only	15
2	Both hands on	Sacral only	15
3	Both hands on	Solar Plexus only	15
4	Both hands on	Heart only	15
5	Both hands on	Throat only	15
6	Both hands on	Brow/3rd Eye only	15
7	Both hands on	Crown only	15
Remember **Do one chakra per day** **The chakras are interlocked and as you work with one chakra it will affect your whole system**			

Week 2 - Hand Positions for the 21-day Cleansing Process

Week 2 Daily Exercise			
Day	Hands	Chakra	Minutes
1	Both hands on	Each chakra from Root to Crown	2 min. per Chakra
2	Both hands on	Each chakra from Root to Crown	2 min. per Chakra
3	Both hands on	Each chakra from Root to Crown	2 min. per Chakra
4	Both hands on	Each chakra from Root to Crown	2 min. per Chakra
5	Both hands on	Each chakra from Root to Crown	2 min. per Chakra
6	Both hands on	Each chakra from Root to Crown	2 min. per Chakra
7	Both hands on	Each chakra from Root to Crown	2 min. per Chakra
			15 Minutes Total
Remember **Do all 7 chakras per day – total time each is 15**			

Week 3 Daily Exercise			
Day	Hands	Chakra	Minutes
1	Start with both hands on	Root then walk up the chakra system as follows: Leave one hand on root, place other hand on Sacral Take hand off root, place on Solar Plexus Take hand off Sacral, place on Heart Take hand off Solar Plexus, place on Throat Take hand off Heart, place on 3rd Eye Take hand off Throat, place on Crown	2 min. per Chakra
2	Repeat as above	Repeat as above	2 min. per Chakra
3	Repeat as above	Repeat as above	2 min. per Chakra
4	Repeat as above	Repeat as above	2 min. per Chakra
5	Repeat as above	Repeat as above	2 min. per Chakra
6	Repeat as above	Repeat as above	2 min. per Chakra
7	Repeat as above	Repeat as above	2 min. per Chakra
			15 Minutes Total

Remember

- During the 21-day cleansing process, as you use the above hand positions, you will release toxins from your body and balance what is occurring within your body on four levels which are:
  - Emotional body – Reiki calms, soothes, balances and disperses negative feelings such as fear, abandonment, anger/rage, rejection or despair
  - Mental body – Reiki helps you to focus and promotes clarity. It reduces memory loss, confusion, and obsessive thinking
  - Physical body - When Reiki is applied to aches and pains, it helps repair the underlying dis-ease
  - Spiritual body – Reiki allows you to connect with your spiritual self or soul and gives you the ability to discover and understand your immense potential as powerful healing energy beings
- Each person will react differently to the cleansing process

21-DAY CLEANSING PROCESS SYMPTOMS AND HELPFUL SOLUTIONS

Symptoms During 21-day Cleansing/Detoxification Period – during this period you may experience some of the following symptoms, but these will clear as a natural process:

- Chills
- Cloudy urine
- Cravings
- Crying spells
- Diarrhea
- Feelings of depression or sadness
- Fever
- Flu like symptoms
- Frequent urination
- Headache
- Increased body temperature
- Increased perspiration or body odor
- Insomnia
- Muscle stiffness or pain
- Nausea
- Tiredness
- Vivid dreams

Helpful Solutions During 21-day Cleansing/Detoxification Period - try any or a combination of the following to alleviate the symptoms you may experience:

- Be sure to do your daily Reiki exercises as shown in the following tables
- Eat nourishing, well-balanced meals
- Eliminate junk food as much as possible
- Enjoy some quiet time for yourself, listening to soft music, reading a book or watching a comedy movie
- Get extra sleep
- Go for a massage or reflexology treatments

- Go for long, relaxing walks in nature
- Have relaxing baths using bath salts or Epsom salt (because salt ionizes your aura it has the natural ability to cleanse, plus strengthen it, leaving you feeling refreshed)
- Meditate (consistency is more important than the length of time spent – E.g. if you only have 5 minutes per day, this is more beneficial than 30 minutes once per week)
- Do deep-breathing exercises
- Reduce alcohol and tobacco products to a minimum
- Drink pure water (6-8 glasses per day) to help cleanse toxins from your system.

"For me, singing sad songs often has a way of healing a situation. It gets the hurt out in the open into the light, out of the darkness." - Reba McEntire

Chakra	Color	Gland	Associated Parts of the Body	Theme/ Lesson	Positive Traits	Negative Traits
1st Root	Red	Adrenal	Everything solid, spine, bones, teeth, nails, legs, anus, intestines, prostate gland, blood, cell multiplication,	Survival, Procreation, Physical vitality, Grounding, Stability, the power to succeed	Purity, Perfection Restoration	Lust, Sexual imbalance
2nd Sacral	Orange	Reproductive Organs (Gonads)	Sex organs, bladder, prostate, womb	Relationships, Emotions, Sensuality, Eroticism, Creativity, Awe, Enthusiasm	Transmutation, Forgiveness, Freedom, Invocation, Mercy, Compassion	Anger, Hate, Dislike
3rd Solar Plexus	Yellow (Yellow)	Pancreas	Lower back, abdominal cavity, digestive tract, stomach, liver, spleen,	Power and Influence, Will, Logical thinking mind, Strength, Wisdom	Peace, Healing, Ministration	Greed, Gluttony, Fear

CHAKRA ASSOCIATION CHART

			gallbladder, autonomic nervous system			
4th Heart	Green or Pink	Thymus	Upper back, heart, rib cage and chest cavity, lower lungs, blood, circulatory system, skin, hands, immune system	Unconditional love, Compassion, Sharing, Empathy, Selflessness, Devotion, Healing	Divine love	Lethargy, Laziness, Boredom, Depression
5th Throat	Blue	Thyroid	Upper lungs, bronchial, esophagus, vocal chords, throat, nape of neck, jaw, jowls, arms	Communication, Self-expression, Openness, Independence, Inspiration	God's will, Power, Illumined faith, Protection	Envy, Jealousy, Personal power, Self-righteousness, Arrogance
6th Third Eye	Indigo	Pituitary	Controls endocrine system,	Intuition, Higher vision, Mental	Truth, healing, Inner vision,	Selfish pride, Doubt, Intellectual

			left brain hemisphere, ears, nose, sinuses, left eye, parts of nervous system, face	powers, Inner senses, Manifestation	Concentration, Consecration	arrogance, Conceit
7th Crown	Violet or White	Pineal	Controls cerebrum, right brain hemisphere, central nervous system, right eye	Spiritual awareness, God connection	God illumination, Wisdom, Understanding Enlightenment	None

"Gracious words are a honeycomb, sweet to the soul and healing to the bones." - Proverbs 16:23-25

THE POWER OF REIKI THROUGH FOCUSED INTENTION

Your thoughts are energy, energy creates action, which in turn creates your present reality; therefore, it is important to think and to feel with a positive focus and intention. This creates a shift in the universal collective energy source upon which we all draw from.

You have probably heard the old saying, "the power of positive thinking", but there is so much truth to this statement that we foolishly take it for granted, simply because our thoughts can and do become our reality, in other words, we are what we "think."

Or you may have heard of groups of people praying for a healing and then a miracle suddenly occurs. This is focused intention working at its best.

How to Establish Focused Intention

- Before beginning your Reiki session, relax and close your eyes

- Take 3 deep, slow breaths

- Silently affirm to yourself, your intention for your Reiki session (E.g. what is your purpose for your Reiki session? See chart below for suggestions)

- Ask for assistance from your Spirit Healing Team (E.g. This can include guides, angels, a universal source or creator, God, Allah, Buddha., DrMikaoUsui and healing masters/teachers, etc.)

- Keeping relaxed you may either open your eyes or keep them closed while you continue with your Reiki session, but listen to and be aware of your intuition - what do you feel, see, hear, smell, taste, sense or just know?

- Do what your intuition guides you to do regardless of the traditional, standard hand positions. (E.g. Place your hands to where you feel you are guided or put color on the area that you feel requires it)
- When your Reiki session is complete, remember to silently give thanks of gratitude to your Spirit Healing Team

With focused intention, Reiki can......

1. Adjust itself according to the needs of the recipient

2. Awaken and sharpen your intuitive abilities

3. Balance the body's energies, promoting peace and harmony

4. Cleanse the body of poisons, impurities or toxins

5. Enhance the healing properties of crystals and gemstones

6. Enhance your creativity

7. Function on all levels – mental, physical, emotional or spiritual

8. Loosen blocked energy to promote a state of

total relaxation

9. Perform as an extremely pleasant, relaxed, holistic method for healing

10.   Relieve pain, stress, anxiety or grief

11.   Support and activate the body's natural ability to heal itself

12.   Support and facilitate conventional medical practices

13.   Support the healing process for animals and plants

14.   Vitalize and purify food and water

15.   Vitalize both the body and the soul
16.   Re-establish spiritual equilibrium and mental well-being.

7 CHAKRA SYSTEM

Insome Indian religions, a chakra (Sanskrit chakra, "wheel") is thought to be an energy point or node in the subtle body. Chakras are believed to be part of the subtle body, not the physical body, and as such, are the meeting points of the subtle (non-physical) energy channels called nadi. Nadi are believed to be channels in the subtle body through which the life force (Prana) (non-physical) or vital energy (non-physical) moves. Various scriptural texts and teachings present a different number of chakras. It's believed that there are many chakras in the subtle human body, per the tantric texts, but there are seven chakras that are the most important ones.

(7) Crown Chakra
(6) Third Eye?
(5) Throat Chakra
(4) Heart Chakra
(3) Solar Plexus
(2) Sacral or Spleen Chakra
(1) Root Chakra

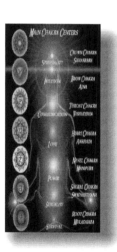

The 1st chakra is called the Root chakra. It is located between the anus and the genitals and relates to the coccyx. The Root Chakra opens downward. When active with vigor, it is fiery red-orange in color.

The 2nd chakra is called the Sacral or Spleen chakra. Located over the spleen, it is sun-like in color and opens towards the front. Sanskrit books always substitute the 2nd sacral chakra with that of the spleen, locating it below the navel instead of at the spleen. My research suggests that there is a danger associated with tampering with the spleen, so perhaps therefore they locate it below the navel. I don't know.

The 3rd chakra is called the Solar Plexus chakra. It is located about two finger-breaths above the navel and is directly connected to our astral or emotional body. Through the solar plexus chakra, we absorb the solar energy which nurtures our etheric body, which energizes and maintains our physical body. This is where our emotional (feeling) energy radiates, particularly our "gut feelings." It glows a golden color.

The 4th chakra is called the Heart chakra. It is the center of our entire chakra system. It is in the center of the breast at the level and vicinity of the heart cavity and connects the three LOWER physical and emotional centers to the three HIGHER mental and spiritual centers. Its color is chiefly green.

The 5th chakra is called the Throat chakra. It is located between the depression in the neck and the larynx, beginning at the cervical vertebra behind the Adam's apple. It starts at the cervical vertebra and opens towards the front. It is also connected to a small secondary chakra, which has its seat in the neck and opens to the back, but since the two chakras are so closely related, they have been integrated into one. Although it has a lot of blue about it, it is also silvery, like moonlight upon rippling water. Blue and green predominate.

The 6th chakra is called the Third Eye? chakra. It is associated with the pituitary gland, which is a very small, shapeless organ about 1/8 inch in diameter located in the forehead about one finger-breath above the bridge of the nose between the eyebrows. Here conscious perception of being takes place. It is the seat of our higher mental powers. On the physical plane, it is the highest center of command for the central nervous system. One half is chiefly rose-colored with a lot of yellow, and the other half is predominantly purplish-blue.

The 7th chakra is called the Crown (Third Eye?) chakra. It is seated in the pineal gland, which is a small organ of fleshy consistency not much larger than the pituitary. The pineal gland is located near and behind the pituitary body almost in the exact center of your head at the level of your ears. The Crown Chakra opens upward, at the top of your head. Medical science has yet to conclusively determine the physical influence this gland has on the human body (probably because metaphysics is beyond their rational thinking mind.) Although it contains all sorts of prismatic hues, it is predominantly violet.

MANTRAS RELATED TO CHAKRAS

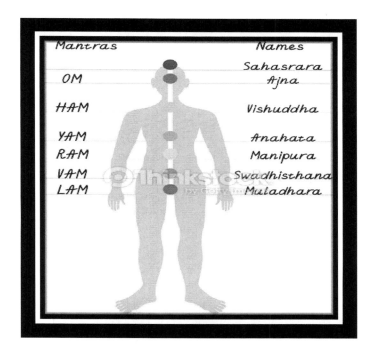

Table 1 The 7 main chakras with their currently popular names, their number of petals or segments, their currently assigned colors, and their traditional Hindu colors.			
Chakra	**Petals / Segments**	**Color (current)**	**Traditional Color**
Crown Chakra	960 or 972 or 1000	Violet or White	
Brow Chakra	2 or 96	Indigo or Violet	Luminescent Blue or White
Throat Chakra	16	Blue	Smokey Purple
Heart Chakra	12	Green	Smokey Green or Grey
Solar Plexus Chakra	10	Yellow	
Sacral Chakra	6	Orange	Light Blue
Root Chakra	4	Red	Yellow

THANK YOU & BLESSINGS!!

Printed in Great Britain
by Amazon

59120974R00043